WORD

OF

MOUTH

2.0

How to Multiply Your Sales through
the Power of Customer Referrals

ADAM MCCLELLAN

ISBN: 978-0-359-49903-8

Lulu Publishing Services rev. date: 2/28/2019

TABLE OF CONTENTS

A NOTE FROM THE AUTHOR

This book is intended to help you increase your referrals through social media platforms. It will guide you through the steps of preparing your social media page to be used for your business, what and when to post, and how to help your clients begin to generate referrals for you. I focus primarily on the solar industry and Facebook, but the same principles can be applied to any direct-sales job, product, or business, along with any other social media platform.

All images in this book come from my direct experience with clients on social media. I have chosen to blur images and last names because of copyright laws and to respect privacy, except where I was given express permission by my clients to share their photos and words.

FOREWORD

With eighteen years of experience selling and managing some of the highest-generating sales companies in the US, I've seen most sales techniques out there, and I've been able to track statistically how they have worked.

When I started with Vivint Solar, one of the first phone calls I made was to Adam McClellan. I wanted to bring him on as a sales leader because I knew the impact he could make on the company's growth with his sales expertise. After bringing him on, Vivint Solar quickly grew into the number-one solar provider in New England and Massachusetts under his management.

Adam McClellan is a veteran sales leader with nearly two decades of direct-sales experience under his belt, both personally knocking doors and managing his own successful sales teams. He has continually been in the top 3 percent of the sales force and, more importantly, a leader and an example in the company. Adam has more than four hundred personal solar installations, and he accomplished this milestone within his first three years working for us. Prior to being promoted to director and then regional vice president, Adam managed the top solar sales team in the industry, which installed more accounts than any other team during the same time period.

With one of the highest NPS scores I've seen in a sales leader, Adam has become a highly successful regional vice president. With more than six hundred sales professionals under his wing, his regional offices are overseeing half of the company's revenue and production.

Over time, Adam developed an innovative training program that utilizes social media to generate referrals that create higher sales conversion rates. This means less operational cost to support his sales pipeline. Adam has the unique ability to transform lower-producing reps into high-producing sales pros that end up sticking around long-term.

Now you have the opportunity to have this program and the benefits of Adam's years of experience at your fingertips. With the success and growth we have seen at Vivint Solar, I can wholeheartedly endorse the effectiveness Adam's method can have on your own business development.

Chance Allred
Chief Sales Officer
Vivint Solar

Chapter

1

Does Facebook Really Work?

In the world of door-to-door sales, Saturdays are the biggest day of the week. Saturdays are like Christmas, but they happen every week! Saturday is the day you turn a bad week into a great week and put an exclamation point on an already great week. Saturday is the day you catch both husband and wife at home, the day you can make sales from 9:00 a.m. to 9:00 p.m., the day you skip lunch because you don't have time to take a break. Saturday is the most valuable day of the week, the day you never schedule appointments. Saturdays are for selling—selling triple or even five times the amount you sell on a week day. Records are set on Saturdays. Records are broken on Saturdays. I *love* Saturdays. Well, not every Saturday.

It was early February of 2013, and Governor Deval Patrick had declared a state of emergency in Massachusetts. A record-breaking storm had just dumped on the Northeast and hit the greater Boston area harder than anywhere in the country. As I watched the news Friday night in disbelief, Governor Patrick announced that all roads and highways would officially be closed the next day and anyone caught driving would be issued a citation. That didn't really work for me. I was one sale short of hitting the incentive my company had given that week, an additional $500 on top of the sales commission. As I went to bed that night I wondered, *How bad can it really be tomorrow?* Regardless of the answer, I knew I would be going out to sell.

More than thirty inches of snow dumped on Lowell, Massachusetts, that night and continued on throughout the next day. When I opened my garage to head out for the day, I wasn't sure my Prius was going to make it out of the driveway, let alone get to the area I was working at the time. Lucky for me the plows had hit some of the main roads, but the moment I turned into the neighborhoods, the roads became single track with four- to eight-foot snow banks on either side.

There were no cars on the road due to Governor Patrick's ban, but it was still a little nerve-racking weaving the Prius through the area.

My goal was to get my final sale for the week, get the incentive, and go home. Selling anything door-to-door is a challenge, but trudging through four-foot snow piles and wind drifts to get to front doors is an entirely different struggle. Homeowners looked at me as if I was an alien when they answered the door. While most were nice enough to chat for a minute, they would notice the snow stuck to my clothes waist-high and politely let me know they weren't interested.

It took me more than three hours to get into my first home and close the deal. It was a quick sale that ultimately ended up canceling a few weeks later in the process, but at the time, I had met my goal. The silver lining from that day was that two other homeowners I'd set appointments with for the following week did end up going with me and were both installed. In hindsight the fruits of my labor really did pay off, but I learned something even more important that day about myself: I had the passion to do things that others didn't want to do or couldn't do. That night as I hopped on our company reporting website, I was the *only* sales rep in Massachusetts to make a sale that day. At the time there were more than 130 sales reps in our company in Massachusetts, and not a single other rep had braved the snow. To do something that no one else had done was something that gave me a sense of pride. In the most adverse circumstances imaginable, I was still able to get it done. No one else did, and I loved it.

Something else happened that day that changed the way I approached my job. While I was struggling through the snow from house to house, I started thinking about alternative ways to create sales. While no one will ever convince me there is a more-effective way to sell a product for a home than door-to-door sales, I also needed to figure out a way to create business while I was on vacation, or even while I was out on the doors. *There has to be a way to generate business that can supplement the sales I create door-to-door,* I thought. An idea started forming in my mind about how I could incentivize my customers to talk about me and my company on Facebook. I had been friend-requesting my customers to stay in touch, but I hadn't capitalized on the network I was unknowingly creating. They say necessity is the mother

> I needed to figure out a way to create business while I was on vacation, or even while I was out on the doors.

of invention, and it took working in an epic snowstorm for me to finally begin thinking of alternative ways to supplement my business.

As I began to reach out to my customers and incentivize them to help me out on Facebook, I also learned about nature of the app. I took note of customer behavior and, more importantly, their friends' behaviors and reactions. I made a lot of mistakes but was a quick study. I kept trying new things—new ways of posting install photos, power bills, and more—to see how people reacted and whether or not it generated referrals. As the referrals started pouring in I knew I was onto something, but the real eye opener came when I received a call one day from our CEO. He told me that he had run into a member of upper management from Facebook at a conference in northern California. He had explained to the guy from Facebook about the way I was using it for business, and the man was intrigued. He let me know that this guy was going to call me the following day to pick my brain on what I'd been up to, what was and wasn't working, and how I thought they could help.

I spent three hours on the phone with the guy from Facebook covering everything I could think of and answering his questions. He seemed completely fascinated about my opinion of the app, how to use it, and why I did the things I did. It made me realize the value I had created for myself, and as I continued to improve the way I used the app I knew it was something I needed to share with my teams. As I've traveled around to different offices to provide training on these principles, the reaction is always the same: everyone wants to try it.

Make no mistake, using Facebook to create sales requires patience, organization, and strategy. It is work, so if you think simply creating a Facebook page will solve your sales problems, you're wrong. My goal with this book is to show you what I've done, why it's worked, and walk you step-by-step to do what I've done. If you aren't getting referrals past 10:00 p.m. on a nightly basis, or anytime of the day for that matter, then you haven't reached your potential as a direct-sales professional. That is what this book will help you accomplish.

I've been in the door-to-door sales industry since 2003. I started selling Winder Dairy delivery service in St. George, Utah, on the weekends in college. As a member of the Southern Utah University football team, I didn't have much free time to earn money, but any day or evening we had off, Steve and Grant Smith (cousins), Nic DiPadova, and I would cruise down to St. George, pick up the delivery truck from the warehouse, load our mini coolers with samples, and hit the doors. *From the cow to your doorstep in seventy-two hours!* This was my first taste of direct sales, and after making $20 per account I set up, I was hooked!

I was living in an unfinished basement for free, didn't have a job, was playing football, and trying to maintain a high GPA. When I sold three to five accounts in a three-hour period on a random weeknight, I was living large! Never in my dreams had I imagined being able to make $100 in two hours. That was enough money to live on for weeks, and it was then that I knew I would never work an hourly or salary job again. I developed confidence by selling an easy product. I could write my own paycheck anytime I wanted, and that was freedom I valued.

Upon graduating from SUU, I was recruited by an old friend named Brett Kesler to sell alarms in Columbus, Ohio, for the summer. What started as a summer job quickly turned into a career when I realized the income potential in addition to the opportunity to travel around the country. At the time, my wife and I didn't have any kids, and we were up for the adventure.

During the eight years I spent managing sales teams and selling alarms, referrals were never a huge part of my business. The product was solid, but we were seasonal salesmen who weren't sticking around in a market for more than four to six months. I never viewed my business as something permanent, nor did I ever make an effort to assimilate into living in the market.

When it came to Facebook, I had never looked at the app as anything other than a social media pastime. It never crossed my mind that it could create business, and to be honest, I didn't spend much time on it.

Shortly after I started selling solar, my paradigm began to shift. I wasn't moving around anymore; we were putting down roots. My wife and I moved to Boston with the intent of staying forever, and because of that, it altered the way I approached every customer. I wasn't very familiar with how Facebook worked and wasn't sure how effective it would be as a referral generator. But what I did know was that if I could get my customers to post photos of their solar panels, a lot more people would see my work than if I walked around town banging on doors sharing my offer one homeowner at a time. The question now was: How do I most effectively get my customers to post photos of their panels and create a discussion that will lead to more sales? Every person on Facebook has hundreds of "friends," sometimes thousands. I figured if I could leverage my customers' friends, Facebook could be a really effective way of generating referrals.

As I started using Facebook for work, I quickly learned from mistakes, but even as I made mistakes it was *still* working. Once I corrected a few simple things, the referrals began to pour in, and, just as I had suspected, Facebook became a highly effective way to generate sales. During my first winter in Massachusetts

(2012–2013) more than 40 percent of my sales were coming specifically from Facebook. As my customer base grew, an even higher percentage of my sales were coming from the app. I was receiving messages daily through my Facebook account from either customers sending me referral leads or random people messaging me. I was getting "tagged" in posts on a weekly basis, and my name was being mentioned in comments on yard sale forums, posts about increased utility rates, and more. I was becoming the expert resource for my customer base when it came to all things power-prices, and it put me in a new position: I now rarely had time to knock doors. The network I was tapping into compounded every time another customer posted about solar. And because the world is much smaller on Facebook, every new customer I created and became friends with already had dozens of common friends on the app, which only increased my visibility and, more importantly, my credibility.

To give you an idea of how effective Facebook can be, in 2015 after being promoted to director of sales in New England, I hadn't actively been selling for a few months. The company had a sales competition that pitted the top sales reps in the company against the four directors and regional vice presidents of the East Coast. Due to my large customer base I was still getting two to three referrals a week through Facebook or otherwise, but I knew I was going to need much more than that in order to make a significant contribution to the team. The competition was going to be Wednesday through Saturday of the last week of June, so on Monday of that week I started reaching out to my Facebook network. After reaching out to several customers and making a few strategic posts, going into Wednesday I had twelve appointments set up. From those twelve appointments I was able to generate another nine referrals for a total of twenty-one new sales directly and indirectly from Facebook in four days. Of the twenty-one new accounts created, thirteen ended up being installed, totaling more than $27,000 in commissions!

Using Facebook allowed me to stop selling accounts one at a time. I was setting up multiple appointments every day and was selling by multiplication instead of addition. As I began using the app to create referrals, I watched for behaviors of my customers and their friends: the way they would respond to a post or comment, the number of comments specific types of posts would generate, and ultimately which posts were creating the most referrals. The great

> I was setting up multiple appointments every day and was selling by multiplication instead of addition.

thing about sales is the game is continuously evolving and the customer-acquisition process is a moving target. Something that works today may not work in six months or two years from now. Sales is a land grab; if you aren't out catching them all, someone else is. Make no mistake, when I began my solar career in June of 2012 I knocked as many cold doors as anyone out there. There is no substitute for being able to knock a cold door and make a sale—it is the core of all direct sales, and if you aren't willing to do it, you will always be mediocre. Never be above the job. Every top salesman I know is willing to grind when the time calls for it. Using Facebook or any other alternative channel is not meant to be a substitute; it's meant to supplement your primary work.

During the next ten chapters of this book I am going to show you step-by-step how to begin using Facebook as a means of supplementing your business. You will learn how to leverage your existing customers along with your newly-acquired customers. I will give suggestions on how to prepare your account to be seen as part of your business, how to introduce it to your customers, and how to get them excited about helping you. I learned the hard way, but I will pass along all the knowledge I've gained so you don't have to. I will show you examples of the most-effective posts and how to get them on your customer's timeline. Most importantly, I will explain the mindset that put me in a position to have more than 90 percent of my sales for nearly two years come from referrals.

By April 2016, there was no one in the state of Massachusetts in any company who had personally sold and installed more residential solar accounts than I had. When I moved from Utah to just outside of Boston, I had never sold a solar account. I had spent a decade selling home security door-to-door and I'm grateful those skills translated to solar, but there were many nuances that I had to learn. As I quickly adapted and learned to sell solar, I realized I had an opportunity to capitalize on the visibility of the product. Solar panels on a home are like a billboard in a neighborhood. I needed this billboard to be seen by as many people as possible and as quickly as possible. Since I didn't know a single person in Massachusetts when my wife and I decided to move the family across the country, I felt like Facebook would be the fastest way from A to B in terms of making new contacts. I was right.

During my first quarter with the company I finished with twenty-six installed accounts, every one of which came from knocking on cold doors. As I got closer to fifty installs, I noticed the referrals started trickling in. Once I hit the hundred mark, five to six referrals were coming in per week, primarily through the work I was putting in on Facebook. As I continued to grow my base and quickly passed the two hundred mark, I had enough referrals coming in every week that I really didn't have time to knock anymore. Keep in mind, I was also managing an office of twenty to thirty sales reps by myself for the first eighteen months our office was open before finally hiring a co-manager. Between running sales training meetings, closing sales on the second visit, shadowing new reps, and going to my referral appointments, I was putting in sixty-five to seventy hours a week and loving every minute of it. I love to work and cannot stand to feel unproductive. There are few things more gratifying than staring at your calendar on a Sunday night trying to figure out when you are going to cold call because you have so many appointments set up.

> There are few things more gratifying than staring at your calendar trying to figure out when you are going to cold call because you have so many appointments set up.

I don't believe in the old adage "work smarter, not harder." I believe in working smarter *and* harder. You are capable of doing more than you are currently doing right now. Your capacity for work and productivity is much greater than you realize. Everyone can sell during prime time regardless of your field, but can you sell at midnight? Can you sell at 6:00 a.m.? Can you make sales while you are on vacation? Do you create and train a new salesman to work for you every time you sell a new customer? Selling by multiplication means you do all of these things. Stop selling one at a time and start selling three, four, or five at time. For every new customer you set up you should get a minimum of three referrals; if you don't, you've failed to work smart. *Word of Mouth 2.0* is about how to sell by multiplication. Now let's go to work!

Chapter

2

Where Do I Start?

As I stated in Chapter 1, I wasn't a big Facebook user prior to moving to Massachusetts. I didn't really know how to use the app, never mind "tagging" someone or creating an effective post that would generate referrals. I've worked with many sales reps who aren't very tech savvy or are intimidated by technology, who have now learned to use Facebook effectively through some simple coaching. If you are already an avid Facebook user or familiar with the app, you'll see results even faster.

These are the types of sales rep I most often help get started:

- Those who don't have an account at all and have never used the app.
- Those who have an account but aren't very active.
- Those who are avid users but have never used it for business.

In addition to these different levels of familiarity with the app, there are sales reps who have huge customer bases but have never leveraged them for referrals or friended them on Facebook. Knowing where and how to start may seem daunting, but it's not that difficult.

> If you don't have a Facebook account and are not leveraging your customers for referrals through the app, you are leaving thousands of dollars on the table.

If you don't have a Facebook account and you sell anything, it's time to get an account. I've tried using some other platforms including Instagram, Twitter, and Tumblr, and while some of these principles apply to those apps, I believe Facebook is by far the best networking sales app available. If you don't have a Facebook account, you are leaving thousands of dollars on the table. Stop what you are doing right now and go set up your account. I'm serious, if you don't have an account, stop reading this book, go to a computer, tablet, or your phone and set up your account. Spend some time putting together a decent profile photo, add a background photo, start friending some people and let's get started.

If you have an account but aren't very active, you are just like I was before I moved to Massachusetts. I may have had a hundred friends or so, rarely posted anything, and spent little time on the app in general. If you are like me, that's ok and in some ways an advantage. You aren't going to have to scrub years of inappropriate posts or photos from your account. You've got a blank slate ready for business.

If Facebook is already a significant part of your social-media life, you'll be able to create referrals much more quickly than I did in the beginning. I had to learn basic concepts that are probably second nature to you. Once you learn the strategy, it will be plug and play.

If you are just getting started with your sales job, I highly recommend implementing my Facebook strategies from your first sale onward. I mentioned earlier that the referrals really started to trickle in after my fiftieth installation. I don't believe it takes that long or that many accounts to consistently generate referrals, it just took me that long to figure it out through trial and error.

Many of the sales reps I work with and train on my Facebook strategies have been with their company for months, if not years, and have large customers bases which they've neglected. If this is you, get ready because your business is about to explode! All of the details on how to leverage your customers for referrals will be covered in the following chapters, but for now start with this: friend-request every customer you have right now. Friend-request both husband and wife if applicable and don't worry if they remember you or not. I don't care if it's been five years since the last time you talked, send the request. If you feel the need to jog their memory of who you are, that's fine. Prepare a three- to four-sentence message you can send via Facebook Messenger in congruence with your friend request that reminds them who you are and why you are requesting them. For example:

> *"Hey Jim! I know it's been a bit since I was at your home setting you guys up with solar (cable, smart home, alarms, etc.), but I noticed we had a few friends in common. We've been doing some really cool referral incentives with our customers on Facebook, so I just wanted to be able to keep you*

in the loop. Hope all is well and please contact me if you ever have any questions or concerns. Thanks!"

You can copy and paste that same message to every customer you reach out to if you like, but from my experience, most of them will remember you anyway and accept your request. Who cares if they are wondering why you reached out, they'll find out soon enough as your timeline begins to sell itself.

If you work for a company that already has a large customer base or you are taking over an area with large base, get the list of your existing customers and start friend-requesting them. Be sure your profile picture and cover photo make you easily recognizable in terms of which company you work for. I always recommend sending a quick sentence via Messenger with each friend request to introduce yourself:

> *"Hey Jim, my name is Adam McClellan and I'm the new account exec in your city for the company. I just wanted to reach out and let you know you'll likely be seeing me around the area working with neighbors, but more importantly I wanted to let you know if you ever have any questions or concerns, please reach out to me via Facebook, email, or text. I realize that if you're not happy, you aren't going to send anyone my way, so I need to make sure you guys are happy. Looking forward to meeting you soon, have a great day!"* (leave contact info)

Adopting existing customers is an easy way to jump start your referral pipeline. If any of them have issues, fix them. Whether it's your job or not, help fix issues. It will build your credibility, increase trust, and will absolutely pay dividends down the road.

To summarize, it's not a big deal if you haven't been using the app or even have an account—that is changing today because you want to increase your sales. For the seasoned Facebook user and sales vet, don't move on to the next chapter until you have taken the time to friend-request every customer you currently have.

Chapter

3

Should I Create a Separate
Facebook Page?

One of the most common questions I get from other reps about how to use Facebook is: "Can I create a separate page for my business?" I've seen several co-workers create separate pages (John Smith Vivint Solar), and I've also denied ALL of their friend requests. I don't like when businesses try to invade my personal life, and I believe that our customers don't either. The reason that Facebook works is because, for your customers, you are crossing the line from "random guy who knocked on their door" to a friend who will become more than just the one-hour conversation during their appointment. They are making a decision to allow you to get to know them on a personal level, and they expect the same in return. As in all relationships, there must be an equal amount of give and take. Otherwise, there is no trust. If you create a separate work page and then friend-request a customer, they will see it's a work page and that you are sending a clear message: you are keeping them at a distance and you have no interest in letting them into your personal life. If you aren't letting them into your life, why would they allow you into theirs?

On the flip side, when you become friends with a customer while using your personal page, there is no faster way to build credibility and trust than allowing them to scroll through your timeline. As your customer sees posts about your family, your interests, your hobbies, etc., they start viewing you as a friend rather than the sales guy. When they can see that you have other customers who have tagged you

> Having a solid history on Facebook trumps most negative reviews on the BBB, Yelp, or Consumer Reports.

in posts or commented on photos or articles you've posted, they can see that you are trusted by others. Having a solid history on Facebook trumps most negative reviews that may be online about your company on the BBB, Yelp, or Consumer Reports. When your new customers have access to your previous customers, you can encourage them to reach out. Your previous customer will have your back. It's a personal touch that cannot be duplicated anywhere else.

The other downside to creating a separate page is that the likelihood of maintaining it is slim to none. Like most things, you'll get off to a fast start, but it requires work, and odds are you won't stick with it. When you use your personal page, you will be getting on Facebook anyway, and now your business becomes part of a routine you already have. Rather than just making few snarky comments on friends' posts, you can also reply back to a few messages, comments, or posts that will help you create more business.

Since a personal page is so much more effective than a separate business page, find a nice professional photo you can use for your profile picture and something appropriate for your cover photo. You don't have to turn your account into a strictly business page, but recognize the perception you are creating as you use the app to create business. My goal with my account is to build credibility and connect customers with prospective customers. Having that goal in mind guides me as I post things that are non-work related and also how I select my profile and cover photos. If making these changes is painful for you and something you are struggling with internally, decide if you want to continue making sales one at a time or if you want to leverage the app's power to multiply your sales.

Customers will trust you more when they know you personally. Let them get to know you through your account. Be authentic, be yourself, and be professional. It's much more effective than keeping them at arm's length.

Chapter

4

Appropriate Posts and Account Prep

When I made the decision to start using Facebook, I quickly realized that my customers were going back through all of my previous activity. I had several customers "like" random photos from prior years, which made me think that I should probably go back through my entire history and delete anything that could potentially cost me a sale. I'm not super passionate about politics, religion, or other polarizing topics, but I am passionate about my business and providing for my family. There is no post that is worth losing a sale, and the last thing I wanted was for a customer to scroll back through my history, see something they strongly disagree with, and make the decision not to go with me. Maybe I'm being paranoid, but when it comes to making sales through my Facebook page, I tend to err on the side of caution.

> There is no post that is worth losing a sale.

Since using your personal account is more effective than creating a separate page, there is a commitment that comes with it: whether you like it or not, you are representing the company you work for and are giving up the right to be a jerk. Before you start friend-requesting customers, take an hour or so and go back through your entire history, delete anything that puts you in a bad or questionable light. My rule of thumb is if I were running for public office, would I be comfortable with what the media could find on my page? If you have photos from a party from years ago that could potentially affect your credibility or trust, delete them. If you just had to bash George Bush or Obama for every decision that was made during their presidencies, delete. If you just can't resist sharing street fights and spring break videos, delete. You're sick and tired of the government giving handouts while you "work your ass off," delete. If you tend to use profanity in your posts, delete it all. Hopefully you get the idea, because guess what? NOBODY CARES ANYWAY.

If you go through my Facebook page, you may fall asleep within a few minutes. It's pretty boring. Admittedly, I'm not passionate about voicing my opinion to the thousand-plus "friends" I have, half of which I wouldn't recognize if I saw at the mall. My posts are limited to humor, family, work, articles about the industry I work in, and the occasional sports post or shout out to a co-worker. You will NEVER see a post from me about religion, politics, race, or anything that evokes strong opinions. Remember, your page is a way for you to build credibility and trust with customers that just met you. Give them an experience with your page that cultivates that relationship, not one that takes away from it. To be clear, creating income through Facebook is optional. If you thoroughly enjoy the platform to voice your strong opinions and incite emotions, then by all means continue to do so. My advice comes from a place of creating income in the direct sales industry by leveraging your customers' networks. The more polarizing you are, the less likely your customer base will be to let you into their inner or even outer circle of friends. Remember, your customer did not know you before you knocked on their door. Most customers have a fear of being scammed by door-to-door salesmen and need only the smallest bit of negativity to cancel the deal. I view my Facebook page as a way to ease those fears, not confirm them.

The reason Facebook works in creating strong relationships with your customers is because you are moving them from a work relationship to friendship. Once you have become friends, if they soon realize the only thing you post is work content, it defeats the purpose of the tool. Your customers will appreciate and trust the friendship more as they get to know you as a person. Photos of your family, friends, activities, vacations, and interests are all great, and while I caution against being a jerk with your strong opinions, you can and should still be yourself.

Living in Massachusetts, I have no problem posting about the home teams. I also tend to stick to funny (in good taste), motivational, and uplifting posts, or posts that will add value to anyone who views them. I may not get the most likes, but I would be willing to bet I've made more money via Facebook than anyone else in my industry. Most importantly, I haven't done anything that would cause a customer to be turned off by me. I tend to play politics down the middle, I never post about religion, and I always stay away from strong topics. Keep in mind, this isn't just limited to content you publish. The posts you like and the comments you make on other posts are all public to your friends. You may not post anything polarizing yourself, but should you make polarizing comments on someone else's post, your customers could see them, and it will no doubt shape their opinion of you. Think before you speak.

If Facebook hasn't been a big part of your life previous to your decision to use it for work, you'll likely have no issues with your past, present, or future with the app. However, most people have been using the app for years, and many people love to use the app for shock value, incendiary posts, and polarizing opinions, or for sharing racy or inappropriate photos, videos, or anything else that may offend the masses. Facebook is a fantastic platform to express opinions or share your interests, but when you choose to use the app as a platform for direct sales, be prepared to sacrifice some of that.

The Clean Up

When I began using Facebook, the only friends I had were actual friends that I kept in regular contact with. I could post whatever I wanted knowing exactly who my audience was and who I may or may not get a reaction out of with any given post. Now, having used the app primarily for work purposes for years, I have more than a thousand "friends," many of whom I've never met, and many who are customers I've worked with.

An experience I had early on with the app taught me a few things. I had gone back for an in-person second visit to one of my customers. We had become friends on Facebook between the first and second visit. While at his house, he made a comment about a picture I had with Jimmer Fredette (former NBA player). The photo I had posted with Fredette was more than two years old at the time, which means this customer had scrolled through two years of my posts checking me out. If he had found inappropriate things in my timeline, it could've influenced his perception of me before I returned. Knowing I wanted to use the app for referrals, I quickly realized that I needed to do a couple things:

- Scrub my timeline from the time I started using the app, looking for anything that could potentially offend. I quickly deleted any of those posts or photos.

- Clean up any and all information a customer could find out about me through the app. Knowing that a customer could do their research on me, I wanted to be sure anything they found would add to my credibility.

You are an official representative of your company now, and while your Facebook page is your personal space, if you are using it to create referrals it's important you understand that your Facebook persona is representing what your company is about. There is no reason to lose a sale over something as dumb as a Facebook post, so don't make the mistake of not cleaning up your page before you start.

Understanding What Will Be Seen

Understanding how the app works is critical to your success, but it can also be a detriment if you aren't careful. Anytime you "like" or comment on a post, that post may show up on any of your friend's timelines. Much like Google, Facebook software looks for trends from users and suggests posts they may like, pushing them to the top of the feed. There are other factors that push posts into our feeds as well, but the point is, the posts you like or comment on may show up in your customer's feed.

As I scroll through my feed, I'm often amazed to see highly-inappropriate content pushed into my feed due to a co-worker liking a post. Your reputation as a professional and someone a consumer can trust can and will be shattered if the customers you are now friends with see that you aren't the same person you portrayed while you were in their home. If they are questioning whether or not to do business with you, your Facebook activity could impact that decision. The posts you like or comment on should reinforce a homeowner's decision to do business with you, not make them question it.

> Your reputation as someone a consumer can trust can and will be shattered if the customers you are now friends with see that you aren't the same person you portrayed while you were in their home.

To be clear, I think it's important that you still be yourself on Facebook. If it sounds like you need to approach the app as if you're inhumanly perfect, that's not the case. Many of your customers will have the same or similar interests and views as you. Your customers will enjoy seeing photos of your hobbies, family, and vacations. It's okay to be passionate about a topic, have a strong opinion, or speak up about something controversial. I believe our customers understand we are individuals and have lives outside of work. In fact, that's part of the reason Facebook is so effective as a referral generator. The point is, it's important to understand you have people watching you now, and if you are using Facebook to create referrals you need to be more aware and understand that anything you post, like, or comment on may have unintended consequences. Ask yourself: If I were running for a public office, could anything on my Facebook be used against me by an opponent? If not, then you're fine, if you have to ask, it's better to err on the side of caution. If you find yourself getting fired up and ready to drop the hammer on a particular topic, just be respectful and professional. Even if your customers or future customers disagree with your stance, so long as you are professional they will respect your differences in opinion.

Posting Compelling Content and Things to Avoid

In an effort to ensure my credibility is never impacted, I've had to resist the temptation to engage in polarizing discussions, arguments, opinions, and more. As much fun or entertaining as it may be to get one of your buddies fired up, it's time to start living above the fray. Do you ever see CEOs engaging in political arguments on Facebook? Do you ever see executives at your company posting street fight videos and swearing on their friends' posts? Would your opinion of your boss change if he/she was constantly posting risqué photos or images of him/her living the life of luxury? Chances are the people running your company aren't that involved on Facebook. It gives easy access to employees or customers, and anything they post has the potential to be taken out of context or misconstrued.

You are a professional, it's time to start acting like one. If you want to be taken seriously, then get out of your own way and stop posting content that discredits you. No one is asking you to become the most boring person on the internet, but many friends I have don't realize they are being annoying or posting inappropriate content. Conversely, take pride in adding value to the friends you have on Facebook by posting inspirational, interesting, tastefully funny, motivational, and compelling content. Most friends I have on Facebook have five hundred to one thousand "friends." That's a *huge* amount of influence and opportunity to create someone's perception of you; don't blow it by being "that" guy/girl. It's important to always remember that you are now operating through the lens of a sales professional. Everything you do has the potential to affect someone's opinion or confidence in you. If something you post or say in a comment affects that, it may cost you referrals. Is it worth it?

Before we get into the "do's and don'ts," one disclaimer I'd like to make is that the majority of the "don'ts" are fine in very small doses. Some of your customers may find them funny—all of your customers have a sense of humor, and I like to believe that most people don't take Facebook content all that seriously. The problem occurs when sales professionals don't know where the line is, and because many sales people are young, possibly immature, have short attention spans, and generally live life talking our way into or out of things, that line tends to be very blurry for us.

The Do's and Don'ts

Don't Be Annoying

- **Over-posting:** If you are posting on Facebook more than once a day, you're being annoying. In my opinion, three to four times per week is plenty. Don't become the friend that no one takes seriously, is consistently annoying, and someone we all just scroll past. If you consistently post more than once a day, it's safe to assume some of your friends think your annoying. Unless there is a major life event happening, posting more than once a day is a no-no.

- **Constant Comments:** Do you comment on every post? Do you have an opinion on every political article? Do you debate commenters you've never met nor spoken to in person? Do you swear in your comments or make vulgar remarks? If you do one or all of these things, you are running the risk of becoming annoying. If you do more than one of these, odds are you are wearing out many of your Facebook friends.

- **Sharing Is Not Always Caring:** Do you share posts multiple times per day or per week? In my opinion, sharing is no different than any other post, so when you share something, understand that goes against your daily and weekly allotment. The posts I tend to shy away from sharing are religious or political. People are very passionate about both and there is more down than upside in sharing anything about these topics.

- **Full of Advice:** Are you the poster or commenter who is full of advice? Do you have a recommendation for everyone and everything? Do you offer advice when no is asking? I have no problem with posting an interesting article on a specific topic, but those who dish out unsolicited advice consistently can become annoying. There is a big difference between offering the occasional suggestion on a post in which the poster is asking a question and being the guy/gal who always has the answer.

- **Tag All:** Please do not be the person who tags everyone you know in a post. A friend of mine once made a joke about a mutual friend by saying, "He needs a 'tag all' button," because he has a tendency to tag twenty to thirty people in every post. In addition, don't tag everyone or even anyone above you in the organization chart unless it's absolutely appropriate. I've seen sales reps tag the CEO in posts that were barely relevant to work. Don't put your boss or co-worker in a position to wonder why you are tagging them in something or if you are leveraging their network of influence to spread your message.

Don't Be Inappropriate

- **Gag Posts:** Posts that are wolves in sheep clothing may be funny to you, but when your retired school teacher customer living in rural America clicks on your link and is re-directed to a zombie screaming at them, I promise they won't think it's funny. You want to start making real money? Grow up.
- **Nudity:** If your post or the post you plan to share has nudity or near nudity of any kind, it will impact the perception of you as a professional.
- **Swearing in the Comments:** If you speak with your friends differently than you would a customer, I recommend cleaning it up. Swearing is not a moral issue for me, it's a sales issue. These suggestions are designed to help you create more sales, to help you improve your credibility. As you comment on your friends' posts they will inevitably show up in feeds you didn't expect. Someone will read them. Someone will think differently about you, or perhaps have their suspicions confirmed.

Don't Be Polarizing

- **Politics:** Each time the political season is upon us I end up "un-friending" at least a dozen people, or at a minimum hiding their feeds due to the annoying content they insist on sharing. Generally speaking, the most annoying people become annoying due to the volume of their posts, and when it comes to politics it's a double whammy. Every political post offends or at least gets the juices flowing of 40–50 percent of your Facebook friends—the 40–50 percent who don't agree with you. Creating any type of angst with any of the customers you're friends with is a bad idea if you want referrals.
- **Religion:** God and spirituality are very sensitive topics for both believers and non-believers. Those who find religion annoying will be immediately turned off by anything religious you post. Those who are religious may not believe what you believe. Just like politics, people are very proud and passionate about their beliefs, and posting about it may affect the way some of your customers feel about you. As I said at the beginning of the chapter, most "don'ts" are fine in small doses and religion is definitely one of those topics. The occasional religious post is great, but if you overwhelm us, your message will lose its punch.

Don't Be Vague/Mysterious/Cryptic/Dramatic

- **Ambiguity:** Is there anything worse or more annoying than the coy, mysterious, cryptic post? Depending on the person and how often they post, sometimes they can be funny. However, nine times out of ten these posts scream for attention, and the poster wants the commenters to decipher the mood or message. It's needy and insecure, and in a world where most of us have better things to do than play your guessing game, it's annoying. Here are some examples:

Rob 3 hours ago My emotions will not be played with ever again.	**Kyle** Yesterday 9:15 pm The one-sided shit is for the birds. Pshh you can have that.

- **Relationship/Life Drama:** If you are the kind of person who airs your dirty laundry publicly, not only is it immature, no one wants to get involved. Do you really think that the 50 percent of your Facebook friends who you haven't talked to in ten years or even met in person give a damn about your girlfriend dumping you? Chances are, the reason she dumped you is because of your lack of maturity, and blasting her on Facebook confirms that. Handle your relationships in private. Seek advice from your trusted inner circle. Every one of your Facebook friends has his or her own problems; they don't need to hear about yours.

Don't Be a Complainer

- **Work:** The moment you friend your first customer is the moment you give up the right to *ever* complain about your job again. You are now unofficially representing the company, so be a professional. Be positive at all times about not only your company, but the industry. Don't bash competitors, products, or otherwise.
- **The City:** Many sales professionals I know have moved to the city they currently work in. I don't care how much you love where you're from and how much you may hate where you live now, don't complain about the city you live or work in. This is the place everyone you are trying to sell to has chosen to live their life. It may be the only city they've ever lived in. For an outsider to come in and publicly say anything negative will be viewed poorly 100 percent of the time by the locals. Find the

value in the area where you work. Find out and share what you feel it has to offer. Compliment homeowners and customers on their town, from the stores to the restaurants to the weather. No matter how you feel when you rolled into town, you better learn to love it, or you'll never reach your full potential. The goal is to become one of them, a neighbor who happens to sell solar.

- **Anything:** If you find yourself complaining, just stop. Stop being a victim and understand that YOU are 100 percent accountable for your results. You are 100 percent responsible for the situation you are in. Nobody likes a complainer and your customers are no different. If they see you complaining about things, they will lose trust in your ability to problem-solve and be a professional.

Do Share Motivational/Inspirational Messages

- **Homecomings:** Nothing will make me tear up faster than a montage of soldiers arriving home unannounced.
- **Motivational:** Memes, quotes, stories, photos, articles, and videos that motivate people to become better are all welcome in my book. Just remember, you're not Tony Robbins; keep it to a minimum just like many of the "don'ts." Otherwise, you cross over into the full-of-advice guy.
- **Overcoming Adversity:** I will stop and look at or read anything that has to do with someone overcoming severe adversity. I'm constantly amazed by the human spirit and what we are capable of.
- **The Prodigy:** I love seeing people do amazing things, whether it's the thirteen-year-old girl playing an incredible arrangement of Hotel California (YouTube), or the homeless guy killing it drumming on upside-down buckets. People can do amazing things and it's always interesting to see it.

Do Share Work Content

- **Publicity:** If your company is publicly traded, you have ample opportunity not only to defend your company but to share exciting news. Don't overwhelm us with articles daily, but if something big happens, get it out there.
- **Customer Success Stories:** Try not to inundate us with customer posts, but once or twice a week we would love to see how you're doing. The best success story is when your customer posts and tags you. There is no limit on how many times customers can tag you in posts about your program. As you begin to have dozens of customers tagging you, you

can decide what you want to allow on your timeline, but if a customer tags me, I want all my other customers to see how it's done and hopefully they'll do the same.

- **Work Events:** This is an opportunity to show off what your company is all about. Your customers are happy to know you are proud of who you work for. They are excited to know that your/their company is doing well. They often draw conclusions about the company itself if the employees are happy and excited. Think about In-N-Out Burger or Apple; they are annoyingly happy *all* the time, and their enthusiasm rubs off on you. If the team you work on has an office activity or your company has a banquet, post about it.

Do Share What You're Passionate About

- **Hobbies:** Chances are one or more of your customers has the same hobby or similar interests as you. Or even better, they have a referral in mind who has similar interests. Whether it's motorcycles, music, outdoor activities, or something else, showing your Facebook friends your interests gives you depth and makes you more interesting.
- **Sports:** Whether you root for the home team of the city you work in or the team where you grew up, I've found that sports brings people together much more than driving them apart. I live just outside of Boston, home of the most-fanatical fan base of any city in America. I've lived and visited all over the country and the people of Boston are passionate. Any time I get a chance to post an article about the Sox, Tom Brady and the Pats, the Bruins, or the Celtics, I do it. You know who likes and comments on my posts? Rarely is it my friends and family from Utah where I grew up. It's my customers. They love it and it gives me a chance to interact with them and continue to build the relationship.
- **Personal Success Stories:** Your customers bought from you because they like you. They were sold on YOU. They are rooting for you to do well and they'll love seeing how you are doing with your job, family, or anything else you've achieved.

Unintended Consequences

As I've previously stated, when you make the decision to use Facebook as a means to create business, you give up certain things, one of which is the way you comment on or "like" certain posts. When you "like" a post it has the potential to push the post to the top of others' newsfeeds. The more "likes" a post gets, the more often it shows up in newsfeeds among friends. A post you "like" also has the potential to show up in your friends' newsfeeds with the notification, "Adam McClellan liked this." The same applies to the comments you make. With that in mind, you need to be more aware of which posts you are liking and which posts you are commenting on.

The hard part about Facebook is people tend to be much braver with their opinions on the app than in real life, but you can't take the bait. I can't tell you how many times I've typed up a big response to a post or comment that I ultimately ended up deleting. It's not even about what my customers see, but also how everyone perceives me. Do you want to be known as the guy or gal with the polarizing opinions? Do you want to put your customers in a position to think to themselves, "I love his offer, his product, but I just can't do business with someone who thinks all gays should stop complaining"?

When you become a professional salesman or saleswoman, it's time to start acting like a professional. Stop liking the photos of girls in bikinis, stop liking the frat party post, stop making inappropriate comments on polarizing topics, and stop ruining your credibility with your tangents that nobody reads anyway. Remember, *this is a decision you are making in an effort to generate more income,* so if your Facebook persona is something you sincerely enjoy and you would like to continue with your strong opinions, then don't use it for work. If you are going to use it for work and you decide to still be immature, you're not only affecting your own reputation but the company and its employees as well. It's okay for your customers to see that you like to have fun, that you enjoy a funny post as much as the next person, but there is a line you between funny and offensive. If you aren't sure where the line is, err on the side of caution or ask your manager. I have sales reps in my offices who use Facebook and I get asked for feedback all the time. I'm always willing to help out.

Summary

Sean Whalen (check him out on Facebook) is a good friend of mine. He breaks virtually *all* of my rules on a daily basis and has more than 200,000 followers on his page. He's leveraged Facebook far more successfully than I have in terms of building his personal brand. He can post something and within minutes will have more than one thousand comments, five thousand likes, and thousands of shares. He makes his Facebook living from being authentic, from being "real" and speaking his unfiltered mind. He recently posted about the Florida school shootings and Second Amendment rights; the post was watched more than fifty million times! While I don't agree with all of his politics, positions, or opinions, I respect the brand he has built. The brand of SEAN WHALEN. The difference between what Sean does and what I'm suggesting is the nature of our business. What attracts people to Sean is his unabashed, abrasive "common sense," as he puts it. Dropping some f-bombs in a post or comments is part of his business. That's right, it's a part of *his business*. It's not a part of yours. People find Sean on Facebook and make the decision to allow him into their life based on the history of his posts and content. Your customers are making the same decision after you (a stranger) knocked on their door. They are going to Facebook to research YOU as a person. They want to make sure you aren't a scam artist, an axe murderer, or worse. Being authentic and genuine will help build your credibility when you are mindful of the perception you are creating and how you want your customers to view you.

Chapter

5

When Should I Use Facebook?

If you catch yourself working on your Facebook page during hours when you should be out in the field, you are missing the point. The way you become a top producer is by working on alternative sales generation during your zero hours, the hours you wouldn't normally be working. I work on my Facebook business late at night or early in the morning. You don't need more than a few minutes to follow up with a couple comments or to post something yourself. It's obvious if you are spending too much time on Facebook since virtually all of your activity shows up in others' feeds. If you like something, post something, or comment on something, it will show up in someone else's feed. Anyone who has an account on Facebook is likely guilty of zoning out for thirty to sixty minutes, scrolling through mundane garbage. Don't be that sales rep. I sometimes refer to Facebook as "the ring" from Lord of the Rings. It can be your greatest weapon or your worst enemy. Don't let "your precious" impact your life and productivity negatively.

Effectively using Facebook as an avenue to create revenue requires discipline when you use the app. Schedule time on your calendar to use it and stick to your plan. By doing this you'll spend a lot less time on the app, and the time you do spend will be more effective. A typical session on the app for me is ten to fifteen minutes before I leave the house for the gym first thing in the morning, thirty minutes during the early afternoon (around 2:00 or 3:00 p.m.), and then another ten to fifteen minutes before I go to bed at night. I try to read every night for at least thirty minutes and enjoy reading a book much more than Facebook, so it's easy for me to put the phone down at night. Since it's a lower priority, I plan time for Facebook around the rest of my schedule.

> Effectively using Facebook as an avenue to create revenue requires discipline when you use the app.

However, I do make sure to actually schedule the time I plan to spend on Facebook in my calendar like any other event. By having the set time in addition to using the time more effectively, I find myself less tempted to hop on Facebook at other times during the day. I know I have those thirty minutes planned out for it at 2:00 p.m. (or whenever fits my schedule that day). You only have so many minutes each day to generate income, avoid wasting those minutes in the black hole of mundane videos.

Chapter

6

When Should I Friend-Request My Customers?

One in eight people in the world have a Facebook account, so the odds of your customer having an account is really high. Rather than asking if my customer has an account or if I can friend-request them, I introduce the app as part of my business during my initial visit. Whenever I pull up photos of other sales I've made, I turn my iPad so they can see me open and use my Facebook account to access the photos. Even more impressive to customers than pulling up a photo of one of your sales is opening up the comments. When you can show a thread of positive feedback it provides instant credibility, and not just with your offer; it shows them you have a customer base that trusts you. Don't ever forget, more than your product, your customers are buying you, so when they see others have bought and trust you it will immediately reduce buyer's anxiety.

Now I've established I have a Facebook account, but I'm still not friends with my customer. At some point during the conversation I will ask if they have a Facebook account. If they do, I let them know that I always end up being Facebook friends with my customers for a couple reasons:

- It is a really easy way for them to contact me They may lose my email or phone number, but as long as we are friends on Facebook they can always shoot me a message if they ever have any questions or concerns.

- It is a really easy way to create referrals. Simple dialogue:
  "Once your system (or anything you're selling) has been installed, what many of my customers do is post a photo and then tag me in it. Our company has a great referral program, so it's a really easy way to share your decision and pick up some easy money! Once we have you set up, I

will actually come by and show you some great examples of what some of my customers have done to generate a bunch of referrals. In fact, one of my customers has given me thirteen referrals from Facebook! At $250 per referral she's earned $3,250 in referral bonuses in less than a year!" (Use the example of your top referral generator.)

At that point I leave it alone and do not ask to be friends yet. Sometimes they will friend-request me on the spot, and obviously I accept the request, but more often than not the Facebook friendship doesn't happen until later.

During the rest of the initial appointment I look for opportunities to use my Facebook app on my iPad to show photos, positive comments, or posts my customers have made. There is no faster way to build credibility with your customer than to show a thread of positive comments from one of your customers. I'll often search the homeowner on Facebook before I leave the home and it will auto-populate to show if we have any mutual friends. The "credibility jackpot" happens when one of your common Facebook friends is one of your previous customers and you can build trust and value from your common friendship.

> The "credibility jackpot" happens when one of your common friends is one of your previous customers.

If my customer hasn't already requested to be my friend, my preference is to send the request when I know the deal is closed. In the example of solar, once I have the installation on the schedule I will friend-request my customer. If I request the friendship too early and the sale ends up not going through, I'll end up being friends with a canceled account, which I'm not interested in. However, remaining friends with a canceled account isn't all bad; I may be able to spark their interest down the road, or, if they change their mind, hopefully they'll think of me.

I end every sales appointment by explaining to my customers how much referrals mean to me. I'll inform them that our company has a great referral program, and knocking on doors, especially during the winter months, can be really challenging. Any referrals they can send my way helps me out a lot. From my experience, customers are motivated to help you if they like you and trust your competence. If they have confidence that you'll do a great job with their friends, family, or co-workers, then they'll feel comfortable talking to their contacts about you. The last thing any customer wants is for someone they refer to have a bad experience. It's embarrassing for them and, most importantly, it won't validate their decision. On the other hand, should their referral make the same buying decision, it will have a compound positive effect on their initial buying decision ,and they'll have the confidence in you to continue sending referrals your way.

Chapter

7

Good, Better, Best

There are three types of posts that create referrals on Facebook:

1. **Good**: you post and tag the customer
2. **Better:** your customer posts but doesn't tag you
3. **Best:** your customer posts and tags you

Let's talk about each option and why they are progressively more effective.

Good: You Post and Tag the Customer

Take a nice photo of the installation and make a quick complimentary comment. Don't be too wordy, just congratulate them and let them know you appreciate their business. Don't make the mistake of posting the photo without tagging your customer. If you aren't friends with your customer yet and you know they have a Facebook account, don't get impatient and post. Wait until you are friends so you can tag them. If you post without tagging your customer, you are defeating the entire purpose of using Facebook as a referral generator. As simple and common sense as this sounds, I'm constantly surprised by the number of posts I see from sales reps who make this mistake.

Adam McClellan

March 23, 2014
North Chelmsford

Panels look great Jeannine & Mike !

The point of posting a photo of your customer's home (installation) on Facebook is to access the hundreds of friends they have.

If I end up not becoming friends with my customer, I won't post the photo of the install. What's the point? There is no reason to clog up your friends' timelines with another solar post that is going to get minimal "likes" and do nothing for you. You'll likely be posting frequently, so don't be the annoying poster; however, if your friends outside of the industry can see how effective your posts are they won't mind.

Better: Your Customer Posts but Doesn't Tag You

While this post doesn't link directly to you, it is still better than you posting and not tagging the customer. Remember, the point is to access their friends, not yours. Your name and company will undoubtedly come up during the comments. Your customer will let any of their interested friends know they can message or call you, which is still effective.

The reason your customer posting is more effective than you posting is that when you post, it limits the comments from your customer's friends. You'll get the exposure to their friends when you post and tag, but everyone can see that it wasn't their friend that posted, it was a salesman. Nobody likes to be attacked by a salesman, so the comments will be limited. Their friends don't know you and aren't going to comment on your post like they would on a friend's.

When the customer posts (even though they didn't tag you), their friends will comment freely and ask questions. They have no hesitation because they aren't worried about a salesman jumping on them the moment they comment. This will generate significantly more comments than if you post and tag. Any dialogue is good dialogue whether it's positive or negative, so just sit back and watch the magic happen.

Best: Your Customer Posts and
Tags You (Referral Gold)

The most-effective way to create referrals through Facebook is when your customer posts and tags you in the post as reference. My strategy is to text or email my customer a nice photo of their home and also send them a few screen shots of some effective posts. Many customers appreciate a little bit of coaching since they have the same goal as you (creating referrals for their bonus). Sometimes I will stop by and even help them with their first post or walk them through it on the phone. Remember, you only get one shot for that initial post, so you want it to be as effective as possible.

The reason this type of post is more effective than the last is because their friends not only get exposed to your offer, but they can see who to contact if they are interested. Some companies won't direct the leads back into the field if a customer calls in through a 1-800 number, so I make it crystal clear to my customers that the ONLY way they get their referral bonus from me is if their friends contact me directly. A typical post from one of my customers will include something along the lines of: *"Message Adam McClellan if you are interested or have any questions. He was awesome to work with, really laid back, and very informative."*

This type of post not only acts as a referral generator but is the most-effective way for you to build credibility for future sales. When you open your Facebook app and show customer posts about their experience with you, it gives new customers the social proof they often want. Each effective post you get from a customer also serves as a template for future customers on how to help you out. Make sure you thank the customers who are willing to work with you and let them know how much you appreciate their help.

Highly Effective Alternative Posts for Customers

There are several ways your customers can continue creating highly effective posts for you after their initial installation post. In fact, the most-effective posts are after they've experienced the product for some time and have a more-accurate testimonial.

Money Talks

In my opinion, the most-effective customer post in the solar industry has to be the power bill of an active customer. When your customers post their recent bills from the power company showing a credit or minimal bill, 100 percent of the time it will get a great reaction from their Facebook friends. The most-effective way to coach your customer through this post is to send them a couple screen shots of customers who have done a good job with a similar post.

If you don't have an example, go to the customer's home and walk them through exactly how to do it. Once you have that example, you can share it with all your future customers. You will be amazed at the results as your customers start to build excitement through their comments. A mature customer base is Facebook gold.

Sometimes customers don't understand how much they are saving, so I'll review their solar account, privately send them some screen shots of their production, and offer them a small incentive to post about it on Facebook. In addition to the normal company referral fee (which I always mention), I've found that offering $20 just to post the screen shots I've sent them works like a charm. My only condition is I give them a guide as to what the post has to include in order to qualify for the $20; otherwise, it's not as effective. Facebook Messenger has a free money transfer service that is really easy and effective to use. You can pay your customer immediately and give them instant gratification. Take it one step further and encourage other customers to act quickly as well by posting about how many customers you've paid for posts. Every time I

34

do this I'll have five to ten customers post their bills. I spend a few hundred dollars paying for the posts, but every single time I get a few referrals from it. One referral more than pays for the posting fees, so as long as you get one, you're golden.

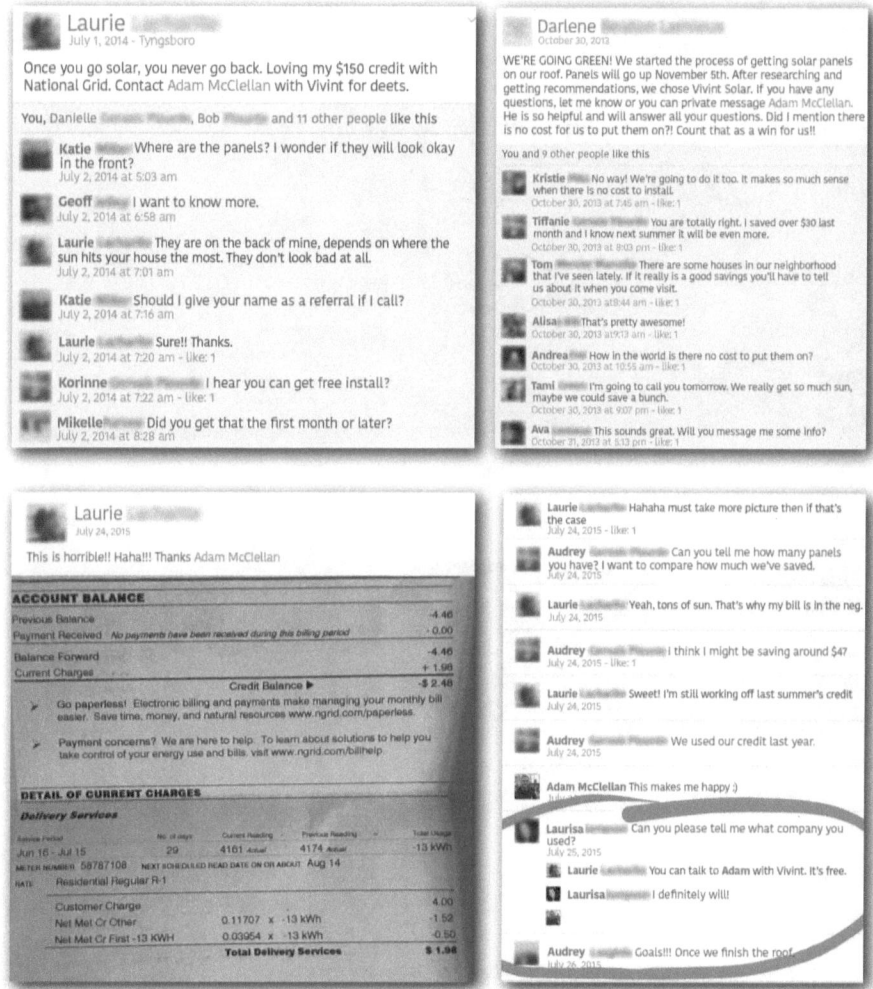

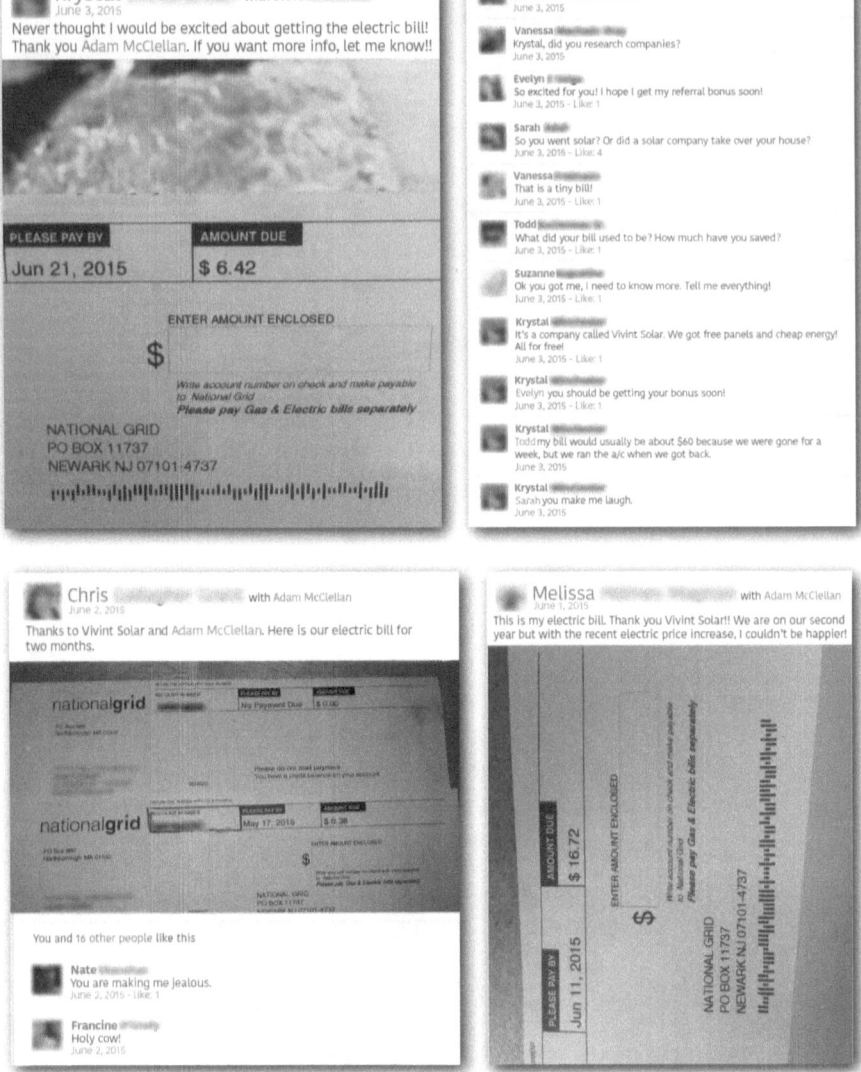

Environmental Impact

Many companies have ways to equate the environmental impact you are having by the number of kilowatts you've sold or installed. If your company doesn't have a way to help equate this for you, there are websites that can help as well. Email, text, or message your customer and say, *"Hey, since your system was installed in 2011 it's generated 30,000 kw/h of power. Did you know that's the same as removing 200 vehicles from the road or planting 2,000 trees! Pretty cool to think you've saved thousands of dollars already, in addition to making a huge impact on the environment!"* If you give them enough good information, they will be excited to talk about it. Customers like to reinforce their decision to any friends who may have been skeptical when they first chose to install. After I send them quality content, I always follow up with a screen shot of one of my customers who has posted something along the same lines and offer the small incentive if needed.

Articles

Any time an article comes out about power prices increasing or what the pollution levels are doing to the environment or air quality, I always post it. The coal industry is the number one polluter in the country and people need to know about it. If there are positive articles about the company or the industry, I will post those as well. You'll be surprised once you have your customer base trained how often they will share the articles for you on their own. Once they've seen the money, they will work for you any chance they get. It's your job to give them the content that's easy to share and post.

Referral Competitions

Something that has worked well is creating competitions for my customers. Once I had seventy-five to one hundred customers I was friends with on Facebook, I realized I could begin to leverage them to compete against each other. I'm a season ticket holder to the Boston Bruins, so I created a competition to see which customer could create the most referral appointments during a time period, and the winner received tickets to a Bruins game. I always require a minimum to win so I don't end up giving away expensive seats for one appointment. During the competition for the Bruins game I received eleven referrals, and the winning customer sent four my way. It was the easiest money I've ever spent.

Summary

The beauty of social media is that it's always evolving. There will be many more ingenious ways customers will post down the road, and the game will continue to change. Be willing to try new things and test new methods, but don't try to force a square peg through a round hole. If it didn't work—meaning the comments and likes were low or uneventful—figure out what you did wrong or how you can improve it. These **Good, Better, Best** posts all came from trial and error on my part. I learned from my mistakes and didn't give up or get frustrated if something didn't work. I paid attention in great detail to the way people reacted to posts, whether it was from me or from my customers. I learned how my comments impacted the dialogue (next chapter), and I quickly realized that a post from me was way less effective than a post from a customer. I learned the value in taking an hour to swing by a customer's house to coach them on how to post. Most importantly, I learned how excited customers were to help me because they liked me and I had earned their trust. It motivated me to want to do a better job with every new customer and to make up for mistakes I'd made with previous customers. When your customers no longer consider you the "solar guy" and invite you and your family to dinner, to a NASCAR event, to a neighborhood BBQ, or to their annual Halloween party (all of which have happened to me), that's when you know you've done a good job.

One of the most important residual effects of creating sales this way is your cancellation rate, or attrition, will go way down. As new reps begin selling in any field, there are many mistakes and errors made, many within the sales rep's control, that cause the customer to cancel. When you get a referral through Facebook, the potential customer is teed up and ready to buy. They've seen testimonials from trusted resources and have confidence in you as a sales rep. They are less skeptical from the outset, less inclined to seek additional social proof, and more trusting of you in general. Why would a potential customer feel the need to research your company online when their most-trusted friends are the ones vouching for you and your product?

While the examples I've given above are specific to the solar industry, the principles are the same regardless of your product. Find exciting features and value for your customers to share, coach them on how to post and tag you, and watch the referrals start pouring in.

Chapter

8

Managing the Comments

A mistake I made several times when I began using Facebook to create referrals was interjecting as the comments started coming in. It's easy to take the bait, but I can promise if you interject and make a comment on one of your customer's posts it will be the last comment on the thread. No matter how helpful you think you may be in answering a question, clarifying a concern, or giving information, any comment you jump in with will stop the dialogue and cost you sales. There are rare circumstances in which it's obvious the dialogue has come to an end or the commentary is primarily happening amongst only customers that I'll make a light comment, but remember, this is your customer's post, not yours. Your customer may even tag you in a comment or text you to jump in on the comments, to which I will politely message them and let them know it's much more effective if they handle it instead of me.

Managing the comments and your customer's response to the comments is my favorite part of generating referrals through Facebook. From my experience, it's my customer's favorite part as well. This is where you become a team and work together. This is part of the experience you are creating for your customer where you can really develop the relationship, shifting from "sales guy" to a real friend.

Managing the Positive Comments

The positive comments are easiest to manage, but it's still tempting to interject on the thread. DO NOT INTERJECT. Typical comments will range from, "Wow, wish I could afford them!" or "Let us know how the savings goes, we've thought about it as well." The strategy that I've found most effective is to simply private message your customer via Facebook if you feel they are neglecting the thread or botching the dialogue. Most of your customers are going to do a pretty good job managing the comments on their own and will resent if you try to control too much of the experience. They'll reach out to you if they have a question or aren't sure how to handle a concern.

When the comments are positive, the goal of a private message is to help them set up an appointment for me. Your customers will usually push the commenters to direct message you or will tag you in response to their friend. The goal is to set up an appointment, so when the referral starts messaging you, keep the dialogue to a minimum and save as much as you can for a face-to-face meeting. I've had several instances where a referral will ask general questions about the offer or product. I give them as little as possible and then defer to the appointment:

> *"Great question, and thanks for reaching out! (Your friend) has been great to work with. It's a tough question to answer through a text, but definitely something I go over with all of my customers when I visit. I typically only need 30–45 minutes and can work around your schedule. Let me know when a good time would be to catch you and your significant other at home this week."*

You'll always have better success answering questions in person than over a text, but if they continue to press I will answer the question directly. Don't ever seem evasive or scared to answer a question, even if you know it won't work in your favor. You will lose trust and credibility. Most concerns are simply a need for clarity, not deal breakers.

Managing the Concern/Objection Comments

If there is a question or concern that comes up during the comment thread that I know is tricky or that my customer hasn't replied to for a couple hours, I will direct message them with something along the lines of, *"Do you mind if I give you a hand with Joe's question about moving after the system has been installed?"* Customers tend to welcome the help and usually expect you to jump in on the comments, which you are NOT going to do. This is where the real fun begins: turning your customer into an expert salesman.

This is where the real fun begins: turning your customer into an expert salesman.

Rather than jumping in on the thread and stifling future comments, a better option is to coach your customers on how to respond. I will send them two messages:

- The first message explains that I will let them know how I would answer the question, but I want them to feel free to add or takeaway whatever they like. I let them know I'll send the answer to the question in a separate message so they can copy and paste it directly from our private chat right to their comment thread if they prefer. I always end that first direct message by letting them know it's much better received if it comes from them and not me.

- The second message will be the actual answer to the comment as if it was written by my customer.

Customers enjoy this bit of salesmanship and the reaction they end up getting on their comments. Suddenly their friends start thinking of them as a credible resource when it comes to the solar industry. Everybody likes to feel smart and well-informed; you're the catalyst helping them out. So long as you've properly explained how your referral program works, they have just as much incentive as you do to create referrals. My experience has always been that my customers gain even more trust with me when I have their back during a Facebook exchange. One of the main reasons customers are reluctant to post for a company or product is they don't want to be called out by a friend or "expert" who questions their decision or knowledge on the product. When they know they have an actual expert monitoring the situation and they can reach out to you as a resource, they are emboldened and more likely to post more for you.

> Everybody likes to feel smart and well-informed; you're the catalyst helping them out.

Existing Customers Who Complain

Something I didn't anticipate after I started generating referrals through Facebook was my existing customers complaining about me or my company publicly. Shortly after my first winter in Massucetts, one of my customers who had been requesting snow guards from me unsuccessfully for a couple months absolutely blew me up after a sheet of snow slid off her roof and broke the railing on her deck. Her post caused a domino effect as this customer was part of a referral network of ten to fifteen of my customers. At the time I was setting her up I thought we would be able to add the snow guards prior to the winter coming, but it turned out installing them just wasn't something the company was set up to do at the time. As a sales rep, there are few things as frustrating as feeling like your customers are upset with you and will stop sending you referrals. Referrals are my livelihood, so having an influential customer actively working against me was going to cost me a lot of business and money.

The first thing I did was take a screen shot of the conversation and text it to my operations manager to see if we would be able to accommodate the customer. Luckily, he responded quickly indicating we could address the issue immediately since we had some material on hand and the timing was good with our installation backlog. The point is, I wanted to make sure I had a solution before replying back to the discussion and trying to calm everyone down.

More often than not, I recommend directly messaging or calling the customer yourself, but since the complaints were gaining momentum publicly I wanted everyone to see that I was going to address the issue head on. First, I apologized for her frustration and then offered an honest explanation of what the situation was. I let her know I would do my best not only to fix the damage it caused, but also the root of the problem by getting the snow guards installed ASAP. Additionally, I let everyone else know that if any damage occurred from snow sliding onto something, they could reach out to me directly and I would be sure we fixed any damage.

As soon as the group saw that I was willing to take them on respectfully, they all calmed down. Once the comments settled, I reached out to my customer directly and let her know the game plan to get her snow guards installed. After working out the details privately, I wanted to prevent this type of callout from happening again, so I let her know how her actions had impacted my business:

> *I understand you are frustrated, and I can't say that I blame you for what you did, but in the future it would impact my business a lot less if you would've come to me privately with the damage the snow had done. I want you to know that I'm your biggest advocate when it comes to working with the company. My business is 100% referral based, and if you are mad at me or the company, that means no referrals. I hope next time something like this happens you will come to me directly first, rather than blowing me up publicly, and give me a chance to make it right. I realize you felt this may have been the only way to get something done, but you have my word I won't make you take drastic measures in the future. I sincerely appreciate your business and will do everything in my power to make sure you have a great experience with us. Thanks again!*

As I've developed lasting relationships with my customers, I've had several who have had major issues with the company or with the systems. When you are friends with them on Facebook, they are less likely to complain publicly about you. Even if they are prone to being vocal, if they know that you are friends on Facebook and that you will see the post, they are less likely to post it. People are generally non-confrontational. If they know they have easy access to you, they should and will come to you directly the majority of the time. If you do get called out publicly, don't panic. If the complaint hasn't picked up momentum in the comments, then reach out to them directly. If the complaint has gained momentum, you'll need to offer a public apology and explanation.

Negative Articles about the Company or Industry

Not too long ago, Channel 7 in Boston did an investigative report about the solar industry and how panels on your home may impact your ability to sell your home in the future. The story featured a unique situation in which the bank the customer was working with wouldn't allow the completion of the home sale unless the panels had been removed. Without getting into the details of the specific situation, the story was filled with several inaccuracies and lacked information from the side of the company (or any company) in regard to the situation.

The story was cause for much concern from existing customers and potential customers. Several of our sales reps were contacted on the day the story aired, and several customers who had started the process with us ultimately ended up canceling. To make matters worse, the station published the story on their Facebook page, and it started to make the rounds.

I happened to be flying home from a trip the day the story aired. When my cell service went live as we landed I had several voicemails, texts, and emails from concerned customers and sales reps. I hopped on Facebook and found myself tagged by several of my customers in the comments where the story had been posted. As I read through dozens of comments absolutely hammering the industry, my company, other companies, and solar panels in general, I thought about how best to handle the situation. This was an opportunity not only to defend, but to educate and create value for my company as a trusted resource.

There were more than two hundred comments on a post that had only been live for a few hours, and after arriving home around midnight, I spent the next three hours responding to every comment. I wanted the commenters to know a couple things: 1) They weren't going to be able to make uneducated comments or remarks without being corrected. 2) As my comments gained visibility, concerned commenters could come to me as a resource to answer their questions rather than an inaccurate news story.

Still, in response to my comments, rebuttals and additional skeptics came. What I didn't anticipate was my own customers joining the discussion defending the company and their experience. Facebook automatically pushes trending topics to the top of your timeline, so with each comment I made, the article became more visible on my friends' timelines and ultimately encouraged them to help out. I had customers posting photos of their homes, defending me personally, defending the company, and sharing their success stories.

There is a fine line between informative and defensive. As I responded to the negative comments I wanted to be frank, factual, and informative. While I used a little more tact as I began the battle, my patience grew thin after a couple hours, but I was still careful not to be condescending. My profile photo has my company logo in the background and if you click on my personal page it clearly states what my title is and what company I work for. As a representative of the company, I knew I needed to maintain a high level of professionalism.

The next morning, I woke up, checked Facebook on my phone, and found I had been tagged in at least thirty to forty comments with more rebuttals from the news article. I spent the entire day working Facebook and eventually got a woman to delete more than fifty negative comments she had made about the company and about me personally. It was nothing I said directly to her, but she insisted on making a claim about the industry that just wasn't true. She worked in the mortgage industry and claimed that every solar company put liens on the homes on which they worked. This, of course, isn't true, and after repeatedly providing factual content within the comments, she relented.

There were several other commenters who eventually stopped as they realized they were misinformed and out of line. I checked the story for a couple more days and, after it lost traction, moved on. During those few intense days I received multiple messages and texts from customers cheering me on, from sales reps letting me know they appreciated me having their backs, and even from a couple of our electricians and installers who were impressed with my tenacity defending the company and industry.

While I didn't create any referrals directly from the article, I took the opportunity to educate. Since that article was posted, I've had at least a dozen customers reach out to me about the concern raised in the story. Others let me know they had questions about it but had them answered after reading through various comments I'd made. Remember, you cannot create referrals effectively if you are not a trusted resource. Your competence increases the speed with which a customer will have the confidence to introduce you to their closest friends, family, and neighbors.

Lowell Yard Sale

I received a text message from one of my customers one day that simply said, "You better get on this Lowell Yard Sale post, the comments are getting out of control!" I had no idea what she was referring to and when I tried to get on the Facebook page it was locked to members only. I told her as much, so she said she would try to get me invited to the page. In the mean time she sent me about a dozen screen shots of what was going on.

A potential customer had posed the question: *Has anyone worked with Vivint Solar? A representative knocked on my door earlier today and seems like a good deal, just wondering if anyone has experience with this company?*

As it turns out, the "representative" was my younger brother who was working in a neighborhood where I had several customers as well. The post had been live for less than an hour and was already sixty-plus comments deep. Some were positive, but there were a lot of negative comments as well. At the time, our customer-installation process was going through some changes, and because we were shorthanded we hadn't been providing an optimum experience for our customers.

I opened each screen shot to view the developing threads and much to my surprise, many of my personal customers were defending the company and me as a sales rep. My proudest moments came as I read my customers resolving basic concerns for curious commenters and encouraging them to call or reach out to me. Rather than jumping in the comments, I felt it was much more credible for local customers to make the course correction in the discussion.

I spent the next hour or so direct messaging my customers who were involved to tell them how much I appreciated the help and to praise them for their responses. Of course, the encouragement from me emboldened them even more as they continued to smash down the naysayers. By the end of the weekend, the thread had more than three hundred comments on it and I had netted three new customers. Few things are more gratifying than watching a negative turn into a positive, but when it's your customers who are changing the narrative for you, it confirms that you've done an excellent job with them.

The goal is to educate and multiply salesmen and saleswomen with each customer. If you sell in a way that is difficult to understand or hard to duplicate, then you'll never reach your referral potential. Your presentation has to be simple and easily repeated. If you bulldoze your way through objections or try to get in and out as quickly as possible, you aren't creating sales through multiplication; you're selling one at a time, and more importantly your attrition is probably really bad. Take the time to ensure your customers understand exactly what they are getting into, make them repeat portions of your presentation back to you and confirm they fully understand. Help your customers understand why it's so important they truly understand how to answer every possible concern. By the end of my sales presentation, my customers know that I expect them to explain my offer to their friends and be prepared to answer questions. I want them to be able to adequately explain the offer so that they do the heavy lifting for me. By the time I get to the referral, they should have a solid foundation of knowledge of what my offer is about. If they don't, it's my fault.

> The goal is to educate and multiply salesmen and saleswomen with each customer.

When Your Friends Turn into Enemies

Now that you've made the decision to turn your Facebook account into a sales generator, there is no doubt your actual friends will have noticed. I played college football and have been in the direct sales industry for more than thirteen years, which means I have a lot of friends who are guys, and guys tend to joke around. I've always enjoyed joking around with my friends and have no problem taking the occasional joke directed toward me, but it can lead to some awkward circumstances with your business.

As I started posting photos of my solar installs and generating referrals, some of my friends thought they would be funny and make sarcastic or inappropriate comments on the thread. Clearly they didn't understand how valuable Facebook was to my business, but I also didn't feel like there was any malicious intent. At the end of the day, I've deleted several of my friends' comments from threads I didn't feel added value to the conversation and, more importantly, might prevent a friend of the customer I had tagged from asking questions or making comments. So long as the comment is appropriate, I have no problem leaving it on the thread, but this is part of the way I make my income and is something I take seriously. If they have a problem with that, then so be it.

Comments Make the Post More Relevant and Visible

Every comment and "like" made on a post helps push it to the top of newsfeeds, so the more comments the better. As you see your customer's post gaining traction, encourage them to reply to the comments. As dialogue increases, the post continues to be pushed to the top of newsfeeds giving it even more visibility and relevance. An effective method of coaching your customer on this is simply messaging them about how Facebook works and how it benefits them to generate more referrals. Don't make the mistake of over-coaching or giving your customers too much of this information during an initial visit or even the first time you are encouraging them to post. If you overwhelm them or put them in a position of too much work, they may end up bagging it all together. Let the experience happen naturally and encourage them with some pointers as needed:

> *"Hey, awesome post about your panels! Looks like you are generating quite a bit of interest from your post with all those comments. Something that's really cool about Facebook is that the more comments your post has, the more visible and relevant it becomes to all your friends. What some of my customers have found effective is that they can stoke the flames a little by replying to the comments, tagging other friends in the comments, or asking more questions in the comments so it continues to create more dialogue. The more comments your post gets, the more it will be pushed to the top of all of your friends' feeds, giving it more visibility and odds of creating more referrals. Anyway, you're doing awesome on your responses to all the comments and questions, let me know if you need any clarification on any of them. Thanks again for helping, you have no idea how much this actually helps!"*

This type of dialogue with your customer continues to build your credibility and trust. I've also found a lot of my customers will start asking me if I think Facebook would be a good resource for their business and if I can help them figure out the best way to leverage the site. Once you are adding value to other areas of their life, you truly have moved on from "sales guy/girl" to someone they consider a friend and credible resource in other areas. Again, customers will not refer their friends to someone if they are nervous about the experience they may have. Nor will they refer their friends to a sales rep who isn't competent. Most importantly, they will not refer their friends to someone they don't like. If you don't continue to build and develop the relationship you started during the initial sales process, you are throwing away future sales.

Chapter

9

Communicating through Messenger

It's important to get to a texting relationship with your customer as quickly as possible. I always initiate this before leaving the house at the first visit. If it's obvious my customer is currently active on Facebook, I prefer Messenger as my primary source of communication. Most sales have a two- to ten-week cycle from the time you knock on the door until the system is installed. Constant and consistent communication is required in order to lower attrition during the process and also for your customer to feel like they are in the loop. While phone calls, emails, and text messages can be effective, I've found that Facebook Messenger is second only to texting in terms of the most reliable and effective way to communicate with customers. The advantage Messenger has over texting is it gets my customers in the habit of using Facebook to communicate with me with less constraint on the time of day in which I send or receive a message.

Think of all the times you've been sitting with a customer and watched them ignore the landline telephone ringing in the background. How about all the times they ignored a call on their cell phone while you've been discussing your offer with them. Think about the way you prefer to communicate. Friends don't call each other as much as they text each other. You could be in the middle of something that requires a high level of your attention, yet you'll still reply back to a text.

The reason I prefer Facebook Messenger is because it's slightly less invasive than a text. Calling your customer after 8:00 p.m. can be viewed as unprofessional, and in my opinion texting or messaging after 9:00 p.m. is where I draw the line. If your client is a member of the opposite sex and has a significant other, you need to be even more cognizant of social boundaries you may be crossing. Think if your wife or husband, girlfriend or boyfriend, received a text from a random man or woman after 9:00 p.m. Solar guy or not, it still can be viewed as threatening. Emailing can be highly effective and is the least invasive of all communication;

however, not everyone checks email regularly and some customers won't give out their primary email address in the beginning of the sales process. The nice thing about emailing is you can do it at any time of the day, no matter how late, and it's socially acceptable. It's important during the initial sales visit to determine how your customer prefers to communicate. If they have an iPhone or smart phone, communication through text, email, or otherwise will be easy. Facebook Messenger is a blend of texting and emailing in terms of its effectiveness. You may message a customer on Facebook anytime, and anyone active on Facebook likely checks their messenger as often as they are notified. The Facebook default for notifications on smart phones is to pop up even when the screen is locked, so unless a customer has altered the default notification they will always be notified when they have a message.

Another reason I like Facebook Messenger is its long-term reliability. During the initial visit I will explain to my customers how Facebook has helped me keep in contact with my customers during the past several years; even if they've lost my contact info, as long as we are still friends on Facebook they can always reach me if they have questions or concerns. I get messages from customers I set up four years ago asking me about billing, a service issue, or whatever, and I'm always excited to hear from them and let them know I'm happy to help. It's really cool to develop relationships with people all over your territory and have them feel like you are genuinely interested in their lives. I don't ever want my customers to feel like I'm unapproachable or not willing to help them. I'd rather they understand I'm very available and always willing to help. You can't create raving fans unless you are willing to go above and beyond—this is an easy way you can put your money where your mouth is.

> You can't create raving fans unless you are willing to go above and beyond.

Don't ever forget the most important aspect of creating referrals is developing a high level of trust with your customers. By giving them easier access to you, being available when they have questions or concerns, and continually proving your competence to them, you will create a constant flow of referrals.

Chapter

10

Selling the Victories

All too often I hear stories from customer service departments indicating a customer called upset they hadn't been paid a referral bonus from a promising rep. There is nothing that kills a referral pipeline more quickly than not paying a customer for a promised referral fee. In addition to cutting off your referral pipeline, you'll turn your customers against you. No one likes being lied to, and to have your credibility or integrity called into question over a promised referral payment is a terrible business decision you cannot afford to make. And make no mistake, a scorned customer is YOUR decision that YOU made by not being organized or following through on a promise that YOU made. One residual effect of your stupidity is that you're hurting your fellow sales reps as well. Facebook creates a web of connections far bigger than we could ever imagine, and all it takes is one customer to post about how their company shorted them on a referral fee to create an unintended consequence that costs other reps in your office accounts they are currently working on. I cannot emphasize this enough, PAY YOUR REFERRAL BONUSES IF YOU HAVE PROMISED THEM. Use the free money transfer feature available on Facebook Messenger, apps like Venmo, Cash, or PayPal and reward your customers for helping you out.

Now that we have gotten that out of the way, let's talk about how to sell the victories in an effort to create more victories. In all sports, momentum is something players can sense and use to create confidence. Referrals are no different, but capturing the momentum is easier said than done.

Updating throughout the Process

When you get a referral from a customer, it's important to remember that their reputation is on the line now with anyone they refer to you. Your customer trusts you enough to talk to their friend, family member, co-worker, or neighbor, and because the referral trusts your customer, they are willing to give you a shot.

Once I've made contact with the referral, the communication with my existing customer begins, which means constant updates throughout the process. The best part about selling to referrals is they don't have to take your word for anything. You can always bring in backup in the form of someone they already know, have a relationship with, and trust. If you aren't leveraging that relationship during the process of selling to the referral, you are wasting your most valuable resource. So here are some examples of all the times I update my existing customer in addition to leveraging the relationship they have with the referral.

- **I've been given a name and number, reached out, and an appointment has been set with the referral:**
  "Hey Jim, just wanted to let you know I reached out to Kevin earlier today and we have an appointment for this coming Friday at 2:00 p.m. I'll let you know how it goes. Thanks again for the referral!"

- **I just finished my sales appointment with the referral:**
  "Hey Jim, just wanted to touch base and let you know I just left Kevin's place. The appointment went really well, and he and his wife seem really excited. They had some of the same concerns you guys had about moving, the roof, etc. If you get a chance to reach out to him between now and next week, I'm sure he would appreciate it. I have an appointment with them next Wednesday to review their design. I'll keep you posted. Please let me know if you think I need to contact him about any concerns they may be hung up on. They seem solid, but most times customers are more open with their friends than with me. :) Thanks again for the help!"

- **I just finished reviewing the design and scheduled the site survey:**
  "Hey Jim, just touching base to let you know the design review went off without a hitch. The design looks great. Hopefully they are really excited. It's actually a little bit bigger than your system. :) I'm meeting with them Thursday evening, so I'll let you know how it goes. Thanks again!"

The idea is that I want my customer to be aware of exactly what's going on with their referral from start to finish. These types of updates continue all the way until the referral's system is turned on and saving them money. When you provide this type of communication, you continue to build a high level of trust. I've found in many cases that customers won't refer you their most-respected friends or family until they see how you do with an acquaintance or someone they aren't as invested in. Once they see how professional you are, it opens the doors to their entire network. Constant communication also keeps you in their minds more frequently, which usually leads to more referrals.

Another important residual effect these updates have is you are creating a team with your customer. I'll drop subtle hints with issues I may need help with or obvious concerns where I need them as backup. Either way, your goals are aligned, so they are willing to help. Plus, they don't ever want to look like they made a dumb decision, so they will sell your product just as hard as you do. When someone they refer ends up going with you, it reinforces the decision they made in the first place, and that's when the momentum really starts picking up.

> When someone your customer refers ends up going with you, it reinforces the decision they made in the first place.

A sales rep's ability to generate referrals varies widely from one rep to the next. Some of our best salesmen get very few referrals and some of our lowest producers create a consistent flow of referrals. The peak performers are able to do both, and the key to success is often their ability to ride and leverage the momentum they've created. Sales volume starts the momentum and then creating an exceptional experience at every turn builds it.

One of my favorite methods to create strong momentum post-installation is to help my customer understand how their neighbors are currently warm leads. Within forty-eight hours of the installation I stop by to check on a few things: How was their experience with the installation? Did they have any questions or concerns? I explain what the next step in the process is for them. And most importantly, I get them excited to help me. I've often found that most of my customers' peak level of excitement about our product is during the initial sales cycle and within a couple days of installation. I want to capitalize on that excitement and use it to get them working for me. By this point I've explained how my referral program works and that I want them to get as many referrals as possible. I'd rather them get the referral fee and tee up a sale for me than knock on a cold door. The sale is stickier and easier to close, but I need to get my customer to move to action. Here is the dialogue I use:

> *"The best part about solar is that it's such a visible product. You guys are going to be surprised by how many of your neighbors and friends ask you about it. Especially once you post photos on Facebook, you'll be shocked by how many people are interested and want to know about the program. It's way easier for me if you have talked to your neighbors first,*

and to be honest they are going to be more open to talking about it with you than they may be with me. Plus, I want to get you as many referrals as possible so you can get paid! Having said that, the best time to talk to your neighbors is within two to three days of when your system is installed, that's typically when interest is highest. So I'll make you a deal. I won't knock a door on your street for the next two weeks, especially if you guys are actively talking to your neighbors. But if I haven't received any referrals on your street within two weeks, I'm coming back to clean house. I can promise you from experience that within the next two to three months, five to ten of the neighbors on your street are going to have systems on their homes, so either you can talk to them or I will. My only condition is that you can't just point at homes and tell me about them, they need to have talked with you and you guys need to do some of the heavy lifting for me."

If you haven't received any referrals within two weeks, you better keep your word and go clean house. I don't like to sell more than two to three homes on a street at a time anyway, so after I sell a couple I'll go back to my original customer and let them know they could've easily had two referrals had they just opened their mouths. I'll let them know I'm easing off the street for a couple weeks so they have another opportunity to create some more for me.

My goal on every street is 80–90 percent referrals. Be patient enough to let the street develop on its own. The only exception to that is if you have a direct competitor actively working your neighborhood as well. If that's the case, all bets are off and it's a land grab.

Facebook is a critical component to help your customers create momentum with their neighbors. I don't expect my customers to go out and knock doors for me, but I do expect them to answer questions when asked and talk about it with neighbors when given the opportunity. Some streets have better culture and closeness than others, but more often than not homeowners are friends with their neighbors on Facebook. As you coach them how to post, this will open the door to conversations, whether in person or over the web.

Chapter
11

The Plus-One Experience

As your customer base grows, the opportunities to exceed expectations are going to increase as well. Customers will constantly be sharing what's going on in their personal life, so you can pick and choose opportunities to make an impact. More importantly, you are getting to know them better, so the next time you see them you can understand and comment about what's going on in their life. Here are a couple examples:

Girl Scouts: Danielle P

I sold to Danielle and her husband, Bob, a couple of years ago along with ten or so of their neighbors. It was a great neighborhood for me, and while Danielle was by far the hardest sale of the bunch, she ultimately became the most influential referral generator. She's smart, funny, and a real ball buster, but her friends trust her, and over the past three years she's referred at least a dozen customers. If I could sell a hundred "Danielles" I would be a rich man.

Shortly after Danielle, Bob, and I became friends on Facebook, I noticed how much energy she was putting into helping her daughter sell Girl Scout cookies. I was really impressed with the way she approached being a mother, and since she had already helped me out, I knew I was going to help her. After a couple weeks of watching from the sidelines she announced it was the last week to order cookies. I sent her a message and let her know that whatever she had left on the last day of the sale to hit me up. Without telling her what I had in mind, she replied that she would.

On the last day of the sale Danielle reached out to me and said she had sixty-eight boxes of various flavors left, to let me know what I wanted, and she would see what she had. I replied back that I would take all of them, to let me know how much, and when I could pick them up. Needless to say, she was shocked! At $4 a box, spending $272 was nothing compared to what she had given me in terms of referrals. It was the least I could do, but she acted like it was the greatest thing that had ever happened to her little troop. She immediately posted about it on Facebook, said I was crazy but thanked me and then put in another plug for solar. It was an unexpected gift, at an unexpected time, and something she will always associate with me.

Since then I can't tell you how many times Danielle, in addition to all of the friends that she's referred to me, has defended me, my company, and the solar industry on Facebook. She's sent me screen shots of dialogue from online yard sale sites in which people had negative things to say, and then her response slamming them back with her experience. Something as small as buying Girl Scout cookies has created an intense loyalty that is hard to come by.

Swag/Bruins/Favors: Jeff H

I knocked on Jeff's door in the summer of 2011. His very pregnant wife answered the door. She is one of the sweetest, kindest people I've ever met, and on that day she was no different. She was interested in my offer, but she wanted to call her husband and run it past him. Anyone who has ever sold door-to-door knows that when a wife calls a husband while you're standing at the door, you may as well call the Pope and ask him if he wants to become a Jehovah's Witness. As Kristen explained to Jeff what was going on, through the speaker of the phone I could clearly hear him say, "You tell that guy to get the f@%k off my property!" She didn't realize I could hear him, so she continued to smile, as did I, both knowing the outcome. After she hung up she said, "You know, I think if you explained it to him he would probably be interested. He's just around the corner helping a neighbor lay some pavers. Let's go talk to him." I was about to pass on the offer given the expletives I'd heard, but she had already closed the door and signaled for me to follow.

As we walked down the street, I asked what her husband did for work? "He's a cop," she replied. *Perfect*. To make matters worse, it was the first day I had tried selling in Lowell, Massachusetts, and carelessly hadn't obtained my peddlers permit from the city yet. In my mind this couldn't have been a worse scenario, and then it got worse. As we rounded the corner, Jeff and six other men were standing in a front yard working in the summer heat, all of them staring at the guy escorting Jeff's wife around the neighborhood. I offered a small wave as a peace treaty as we approached and remained as confident as possible. While being a little standoffish in the beginning, Jeff turned out to be a total stud. Like most people in the Northeast, he has a hard-candy shell, but is soft in the middle.

Long story short, after we installed Jeff's house I made a point of stopping by regularly with hats and other swag for his ten-year-old boy and him. Jeff loves to chat in the front yard on summer nights, and any time I was in the area I made a point to swing by. The referrals quickly started pouring in, and as they poured in I continued to reward Jeff with things besides money. He refused to take any money from me, so I sent him and his son to front row seats at a Boston Bruins game. One weekend my family and I were in Boston's North End, and after dinner we stopped by the famous Mike's Pastry. I remembered that Kristen is a huge Mike's Pastry fan, so I grabbed her a half-dozen cannoli's and dropped them off on our way home.

Do a good enough job with your customers and your company swag will end up in family photos.

As our friendship has developed over the last several years, Jeff has given me tickets to the NASCAR event in New Hampshire. He invites my wife and I to his annual Halloween party, and we take our kids to Jeff's house every year to trick or treat because he takes so much pride in his decorations. I even asked Jeff to help me move some things after we purchased our home, and he was excited to help.

The point is, when we moved to the greater Boston area I approached my job with the mentality that I was going to have multiple opportunities every day to create new relationships and new friendships. I made a point of thinking about each new sale as a new friend that I would be interacting with for years to come. When you approach each new customer with this mentality, you tend to treat them differently. I handle their concerns with more care, and I find myself looking for opportunities to serve.

Boston Red Sox: Diane N

On the day I knocked on Diane's door, the first thing I saw was the Jacoby Ellsbury jersey T-shirt she was wearing. While Ellsbury was beloved by Sox-faithful fans while he played for Boston, just weeks prior he had signed with the New York Yankees. No greetings, no hellos, the first thing out of my mouth was, "Are you serious with that Ellsbury shirt?!" She started laughing and acknowledged the error in her ways. I told her that the next time I saw her I was getting her a more respectable shirt, then proceeded into my door approach.

I ended up starting the process with Diane that day, and after our engineering team had created her solar design, I scheduled an appointment with her to review it. On my way to the appointment, I stopped by Sports Authority and found a Dustin Pedroia replica jersey T-shirt that I could use to replace the Ellsbury shirt. As Diane answered the door I held out the T-shirt for her to see I had stuck to my word. She was shocked by the kind gesture and started laughing, then gave me a hug. Needless to say, the appointment went smoothly and was over within thirty minutes.

As we chatted in the front yard after the appointment, one of her neighbors pulled into the driveway next door. Diane shouted over to her if she wanted solar on her home, and the neighbor was interested. I made my way over and started talking with her and was eventually invited inside to start the process. While I was inside the neighbor's house, Diane began knocking on all of her other neighbor's doors and by the time I came out about forty minutes later, she had three more neighbors interested!

What started as one sale turned into five because I had motivated a customer enough to help me. One kind gesture gave her the confidence in me as a salesman to talk to all of her neighbors. Once Diane's system was installed, she started posting about it on Facebook without me prompting her. She's talked about me to her coworkers, friends, and family members and has ultimately created more than a dozen referrals for me.

Paying It Forward

In addition to exceeding the normal customer experience, I constantly look for opportunities to pay it forward. Here are a few ideas:

- Anytime I sell to a homeowner who is a business owner or even manager for a company, I will leave them a positive review on Yelp. I know how influential those reviews can be for my company, so it's important to strike first and leave them a nice review. More often than not, the customer will see it and do the same in return for you without being prompted.

- One of my favorite things to talk about while in homes is local restaurants. After writing down a couple of the customer's recommendations, I've made a habit of going to a suggested restaurant, taking my photo with the food or in front of the sign, and then texting my customer the photo thanking them for the solid recommendation. It shows I trusted their judgement and also have something else in common with them to talk about next time I visit.

- When I first started selling solar, I had fifty to sixty installs by the time my first Christmas came around. I wanted to do something nice for my customers, so I drove around to each home and took a really nice photo of the house with the solar array. I bought some cheap frames and printed photos to put in them. In the corner of each photo I added the company logo and some stats about the system: date installed, size, estimated annual savings, etc. I then hand-delivered them a few days before Christmas along with five business cards each. I told them they could pay for Christmas with some referrals! The gesture didn't create immediate referrals, but it was one more action that eventually created a reaction.

Summary

These examples aren't outliers. This is the type of experience I try to create for all of my customers, and being friends with them on Facebook makes it even easier to keep tabs. It doesn't take much to create a plus-one experience. A $30 T-shirt, some company swag, buying a few boxes of Girl Scout cookies, liking or commenting on their posts—it all helps. Look for opportunities to wow your customers beyond what they expect from you. Your customers expect to have a great experience with your company and product, that's why they are going with you. What they don't expect is a salesman who answers questions from a Facebook Message, email, or text at any time of the day. What they don't expect is for you to remember their birthday. What they don't expect is for you to remember the anniversary date on which you set up their account.

I'm often asked, "How do you get so many referrals?" The answer is simple: I create the experience that I would want as a customer, and I make myself easily accessible at all times. Couple that with working hard and smart, and I get large results.

Don't get discouraged if you don't get the results you want after one post, or even after one customer post. You never know which customer will strike gold for you.

You never know which customer is viewed by their friends as the expert. As you continue to work hard and smart, the referrals will come. And soon you'll be trying to figure out when you are going to have time to knock because you are juggling so many appointments. There is nothing more fun as a salesman than hustling from referral to referral and connecting with people with common contacts. Your web of connections grows and so do your referrals. Multiply your efforts by making Facebook an integral part of your business. When you wake up on a Monday morning and have five to eight referral appointments on your calendar in addition to follow-up visits and time for prospecting new customers, direct sales can become the most fun and lucrative job you'll ever have.

Good luck!

ABOUT THE AUTHOR

Adam McClellan has been a dynamic leader in the direct sales industry for more than fifteen years. In 2004, upon graduating from Southern Utah University with a successful college-football career and Magna Cum Laude honors, he began his sales career at Pinnacle Security selling ADT home security systems. Adam finished his first year at Pinnacle among the top new sales reps in the company and was quickly promoted first to district manager and then regional manager, where he recruited and led top teams for the next nine years in the home security space.

Under the direction of Vivint Solar CSO, Chance Allred, and Vivint, Inc. founder and CEO, Todd Pederson, Adam joined Vivint Solar in 2012. He relocated from Utah to Boston, Massachusetts, in an effort to grow Vivint Solar on the East Coast by opening the second office on the East Coast and third office overall in the fledgling company.

Adam quickly grew his market by personally selling and installing more than four hundred customers, and his team became the number-one-installing team in the solar industry. Within two years Vivint Solar's New England Region was born, and the territory grew to more than 150 sales reps and eight teams of district managers and sales managers, installing more than 22,000 customers in the New England area. Training sales reps on his methods of generating referrals has become a core staple to the success of the company. With one of the highest closing ratios in company history, Adam attributes much of his success to his ability to encourage self-generated referrals. More than 80 percent of his 400+ installed customers have come fromw self-generated referrals.

Adam currently resides in the greater Boston area and works as the regional vice president of the East Coast for Vivint Solar, managing more than four hundred sales managers that generate more than one hundred megawatts of installed customers annually. For the first time, he is sharing the secrets of his success with direct sellers outside of Vivint Solar because he believes in paying it forward. Change your sales trajectory today and start learning how to multiply your business with the power of referrals!

www.ingramcontent.com/pod-product-compliance
Lightning Source LLC
Chambersburg PA
CBHW021021180526
45163CB00005B/2054